VERY LIKE A WHALE

Other Plays by John Osborne

★

Very Like a Whale

by

JOHN OSBORNE

FABER AND FABER
3 Queen Square
London

First published in 1971
by Faber and Faber Limited
3 Queen Square London WC1
Printed in Great Britain by
Latimer Trend & Co Ltd Plymouth

ISBN 0 571 09628 X (*Hard Bound Edition*)

ISBN 0 571 09689 1 (*Paper Covers*)

List of Characters

SIR JOCK
LADY MELLOR
MARIO
CHAUFFEUR: TOM
AMERICAN GUESTS
LADY JOURNALIST
TED WILLIAMS
STEPHEN GRAIN
TOURIST
TOURIST'S WIFE
PILOT
CHAIRMAN
GIRL ON ROSTRUM
FACTORY WORKERS

SMALL GIRL (MELLORS'
    DAUGHTER)
POLICEMAN
STUDENT
JAN
AIRLINE OFFICIAL
HEALTH OFFICIAL
CAB DRIVER
SON
BARBARA
WAITER
STAR SPEAKER
TV INTERVIEWER

1. INT. LUXURIOUS EXECUTIVE OFFICE DAY

JOCK MELLOR, *about forty-four, is looking at himself in full-length mirror. He is wearing morning dress and looking rather slim. His* SECRETARY *hands him his grey topper. He puts it on and grimaces.*

SECRETARY: No, this way, surely. For you . . .
    (*She rearranges it for him. He looks and grins.*)
JOCK: Not bad, I suppose.
SECRETARY: Not bad! You look quite marvellous.
JOCK: Ridiculous outfit.
SECRETARY: Not on you.
JOCK: Who on earth wears them? Not me.
SECRETARY: Well, you make it into something else.
JOCK: Like what?
SECRETARY: Oh, I don't know. Courtly.
JOCK: Courtly. With trousers this width? And braces? And——
SECRETARY: All right, you *don't* look slim and lean and full of
    life. You look smug, a flatulent and middle-road, fair
    mileage whizz kid.
JOCK: I'm sorry, I didn't mean to be churlish.
SECRETARY: At least, don't be churlish when they lay the sword
    on your shoulder or whatever happens. It's too late by that
    time.
JOCK: I just thought I looked ridiculous.
SECRETARY: You do.
JOCK: Yes, you're right. That's exactly what I look.
SECRETARY: But not as ridiculous as some. In fact—hardly at all.
JOCK: Thank you.
SECRETARY: I won't wish you luck. After all, you've done *your*
    part.

JOCK: *My* part . . .

SECRETARY: The car is downstairs. You'd better be off. You're picking up your wife and Myra on your way . . .

JOCK: I thought they were coming here.

SECRETARY: No. She wanted you to pick *her* up.

JOCK: But it's not *on* the way.

SECRETARY: She insisted.

JOCK: Well . . .

SECRETARY: You do look, in fact, very remarkable. No—don't spoil it with false humility. You probably *are* quite remarkable. It's about time your country realized it and said so—even if it's only this.

JOCK: It's all a terrible . . .

SECRETARY: Mistake. Exactly. It all is. Will you go straight home for the party?

JOCK: I suppose so. I dread it.

SECRETARY: Never mind. It won't last long.

JOCK: No. You *will* come?

SECRETARY: I don't think Mrs.—Lady Mellor will be heart-broken if I don't.

JOCK: Please do. *I* want you to come.

SECRETARY: Why?

JOCK: Why? Because you should.

SECRETARY: Why? *Should* I? *Should* anyone?

JOCK: No. You're quite right. (*He leans forward and kisses her lightly.*)
Well . . .

SECRETARY: See your topper's on right when they photograph you.

JOCK: What?

SECRETARY: They always do. You know—afterwards.

JOCK: I'll do my best.

SECRETARY: You always do.

JOCK: No. I don't actually.

SECRETARY: That's a different decision. And stand up straight.

JOCK: O.K., Nanny. See you with Christopher Robin.

2. INT. OFFICE   DAY
SECRETARY *watches* SIR JOCK *get into chauffeur-driven Bentley.*

3. EXT. OUTSIDE BELGRAVIA HOUSE   DAY
LADY MELLOR *and* MYRA *are assisted into the car. She is rather tense. The child is quiet.*

4. INT. BENTLEY   DAY
Car moves off. LADY MELLOR *arranges her hat.*
LADY MELLOR: Thought you weren't coming.
JOCK: So did I.
LADY MELLOR: That *would* have been nice. Well: good luck, I
    suppose. (*Clasps his hand.*)
JOCK: Thank you.
LADY MELLOR: Say, "Good luck, Daddy."
MYRA: Good luck.
JOCK: Thank you. Both of you.
    (*They approach the memorial to Queen Victoria opposite
    Buckingham Palace. His wife squeezes his hand.*)

5. EXT. BUCKINGHAM PALACE YARD   DAY
JOCK MELLOR *poses with his wife and child for photographers.
Freeze etc.*

6. *Photographs of* SIR JOCK, *etc., with caption* "EXPORT 'KING'
HONOURED BY QUEEN".

7. *Credits over photograph.*

8. INT. C.U. MELLORS' BEDROOM   EVENING
*Television set. The frozen picture of the family outside Buckingham
Palace becomes animate.*
ANNOUNCER (*V.O.*): At the next conference. . . . And now,
    something nearer home and more cheering. Sir Jock Mellor,
    leading industrialist, named "King Export" for the Year,
    and one of the most forceful figures named in the New
    Year's Honours List went to Buckingham Palace today to
    be honoured by the Queen . . .

(*Pull back to* JOCK *tying his tie.*)

JOCK: Forceful! I can't button my collar.

LADY MELLOR: Sh! Don't panic.

JOCK: About what?

ANNOUNCER: Sir Jock was accompanied by his wife and young daughter Moira.

JOCK: Myra, not Moira.

LADY MELLOR: Never mind. She got *some* mention.

JOCK: It's a rotten name, anyway. Why did we choose it? You can't even remember it.

LADY MELLOR: You've got to make *some* choice.

JOCK: Not necessarily.

LADY MELLOR: That sounds like a joke.

JOCK: It is. About being Jewish as I remember.

LADY MELLOR: It usually is with you. Can you do up this last bit.

(*He limps over to the back of her back.*)

JOCK: All this money—why on earth can't . . .

LADY MELLOR: . . . they make a dress that doesn't bust some poor bastard's male eyeballs trying to do it up . . .

JOCK: Yes, exactly . . .

LADY MELLOR: Cheer up, Sir Jock.

JOCK: Oh, belt up.

LADY MELLOR: Captains of Industry don't say "belt up".

JOCK: Don't they—*Lady* Mellor?

LADY MELLOR: Oh, it sounds awful. I think I'll have to get it changed.

JOCK: I must be an Admiral of Industry at least.

LADY MELLOR: Well, Captains or Admirals—they take their fingers out.

(*Door bell rings.*)

JOCK: Oh, God—someone's early.

LADY MELLOR: Never mind.

JOCK: Damn them. They're *ten* minutes early. Must be Americans.

LADY MELLOR: Give them a drink. It's not important.

JOCK: No. You're right. It's not.

12

(*She turns off the television set.*)

It's just—oh, well.

LADY MELLOR: A waste of time? Yes. I don't know what time well spent really might be . . . One can only spend so much—like money. If you know what I mean.

JOCK: No. I don't. I don't think *you* do. I think I know what perhaps you ought to mean.

LADY MELLOR: Complicated . . . I feel so alone . . .

JOCK: One always does.

LADY MELLOR: Yes. Sorry.

JOCK: Don't be.

LADY MELLOR: I'm not.

JOCK: No. Well, nothing is more lonely than the thought of seventy or eighty people about to ring your door bell.

LADY MELLOR: You didn't tell me *not* to ask them, you know.

JOCK: I know. (*He kisses her.*)

LADY MELLOR: Try . . .

JOCK: Not to be too long. I've just broken my shoelaces.

LADY MELLOR: That's all! Thank you.

JOCK: For what?

LADY MELLOR: The kiss.

JOCK: Irony will get you nowhere. The House of Lords perhaps.

LADY MELLOR: For everything.

JOCK: Yes. You could still make a Peeress.

LADY MELLOR: See you.

JOCK: See you.

9. INT. FRONT DOOR   MELLORS' HOUSE   EVENING

SIR JOCK'S P.O.V. *looking down into the hall from the top of the stairs.* TWO GUESTS *are being received by the* "MAN" *of the couple who live in the house,* MARIO. JOCK *retreats back into the bedroom. His* WIFE *is still getting ready, peering at her eyelashes as she fixes them on.*

JOCK: My God—someone *has* arrived!

LADY MELLOR: So?

JOCK: What'll we do?

LADY MELLOR: Go down, of course.

13

JOCK: But they're *early*.

LADY MELLOR: Someone always is. You must know that by now.

JOCK: They *must* be Americans. Do you think Mario or
whatever his name is will give them a drink?

LADY MELLOR: I doubt it. Even if they ask for it. Go and talk
to them yourself.

JOCK: What about you?

LADY MELLOR: I'll be five minutes. Oh, go on.

JOCK: A man's five minutes or a woman's?

LADY MELLOR: Go on and don't be helpless.

JOCK: I'm not exactly helpless.

LADY MELLOR: No. We're all told repeatedly how brilliant and
driving you are. And how you've been knighted for it. So
give some early Americans a drink.

JOCK: They'll want damned martinis.

LADY MELLOR: Mario can just about manage that. If you tell
him loudly and slowly. Now get along. They speak
English, you know.

JOCK: Not really. Damn. . . .

LADY MELLOR: On your way—Sir Jock.

JOCK: Thanks—Lady M.

LADY MELLOR: *I* wasn't *able* to refuse.

JOCK: Poor old thing. You can still call yourself Mrs.

LADY MELLOR: Then they won't know who I am. I'm a part of
you, remember? Me. Part of the package. Now don't keep
them waiting any longer. They'll think you have even less
manners than you have.

JOCK: It was your idea.

LADY MELLOR: What?

JOCK: The party.

LADY MELLOR: It's a bit late for that.

JOCK: I hate these things. You actually enjoy them.

LADY MELLOR: I like to see a few people.

JOCK: People!

LADY MELLOR: *Are* you going?

JOCK: Well, it's all pretty vulgar.

LADY MELLOR: You mean *I'm* pretty vulgar.

14

JOCK: I didn't say that and I didn't mean that.

LADY MELLOR: Well, *you* are, anyway. Very.

JOCK: Thanks.

LADY MELLOR: You're welcome. You always say you like the truth.

JOCK: If I think it's the truth and not prejudice. Or bitchiness.

LADY MELLOR: You're pretty good in that line yourself. Men always are.

JOCK: Oh—*men*!

LADY MELLOR: Yes, men. You may not be a great example but I suppose you just about qualify. . . .

JOCK: All ready to enjoy yourself?

LADY MELLOR: Sure. As much as ever I do.

JOCK: Well, I suppose I'll welcome our unwelcome guests. See if I can't pour a martini down her great front.

LADY MELLOR (*interested*): What's she wearing?

JOCK: An aggressive, gaudy, big-arsed, damn-you-you-can't-do-me-down, I'm-a-*woman* trouser suit.

LADY MELLOR: Good luck then.

JOCK: Thanks—for everything.

(*He leaves her staring at her hair-piece.*)

10. INT. MELLORS' DRAWING ROOM   EVENING

The AMERICAN COUPLE *are talking self-consciously while* MARIO *stands smirking and useless.*

JOCK: How nice to see you.

AMERICAN: I think we're probably a little early.

JOCK: Not at all. Have a drink before everyone else arrives. Martinis?

AMERICAN: A little scotch and water please. My wife drinks bourbon.

AMERICAN WIFE: On the rocks, please.

JOCK: Hear that, Mario?

MARIO (*not moving*): Sir?

JOCK: One scotch and water and a bourbon on the rocks.

(*Pause while* MARIO *fumbles with drinks.*)

AMERICAN: Well—Sir Jock—congratulations.

15

JOCK: Thanks. . . . And how's the good old U.S.A?

11. INT. MELLORS' SITTING ROOM EVENING

It is now packed with people standing with glasses and cigarettes. Very difficult to catch much of what is being said anywhere. JOCK *is trying to be polite to an oddly dressed* LADY JOURNALIST; *all* light.

L. JOURNALIST: You're bored, aren't you?

JOCK: What's that? Sorry, I can't hear very well.

L. JOURNALIST: I say you're bored.

JOCK: Not really. It's not exactly a host's privilege.

L. JOURNALIST: But you're still bored. . . . What's it feel like?

JOCK: Boredom? Oh, daily experience. Like rheumatism. I have it in my hands. Here.

L. JOURNALIST: You know what I mean.

JOCK: I don't know what you mean. I don't know you for a start and I know less and less what anybody means.

L. JOURNALIST: You're a very melancholy man, aren't you?

JOCK: Am I? I suppose you're a dab student of personality?

L. JOURNALIST: For someone famed for drive and initiative. Form of escape?

JOCK: Very likely. (*He is looking for an escape route.*)

L. JOURNALIST: Do *I* bore you?

JOCK: Somewhat. But I don't suppose you would ever bore me more than I bore myself.

L. JOURNALIST: Are you looking for someone?

JOCK: Am I. . . ? No. . . . At least, I was just . . .

L. JOURNALIST: Are you faithful to your wife?

JOCK: None of your business. Whatever your name is.

L. JOURNALIST: You know what my name is. You know your press relations. Everyone says you're not.

JOCK: Everyone doesn't *know*. Because everyone is no-one who never actually witnesses anything.

L. JOURNALIST: Oh, come *on*.

JOCK: You think I'm your property. Well I'm not. I invented myself.

L. JOURNALIST: So you say. Why did you ask me to your party?

16

JOCK: I didn't. My wife always mistakes Barracudas for big fish. Why did you come? I can't believe *you're* enjoying yourself.

L. JOURNALIST: I don't expect to. Do you enjoy selling machinery?

JOCK: I did once.

L. JOURNALIST: What I mean is: this knighthood. Why did you accept it?

JOCK: Why not?

L. JOURNALIST: I'd expected a smoother evasion than that.

JOCK: My evasion device is not what it was. You must be accustomed to disappointments.

L. JOURNALIST: O.K., Sir Jock. Have it your way.

JOCK: I don't see why I shouldn't try. Do you?

L. JOURNALIST: You seem to manage.

JOCK: Excuse me——

L. JOURNALIST: You see somebody.

JOCK: Yes, thankfully. A sort of kindly face.

L. JOURNALIST: Sentimental with it. . . . Why do you wear that ring?

JOCK: My wife gave it to me. And I like it. Why are you wearing that bizarre outfit? With an arse like yours, you should be more reticent.

L. JOURNALIST: My husband likes it.

JOCK: Indeed. No doubt you've asked him?

L. JOURNALIST: You don't like successful women, do you? That's why you divorced your other wife.

JOCK: I don't like freaks. Are you old-fashioned drunk or on the hard stuff?

L. JOURNALIST: None of *your* business.

JOCK: Quite. Have fun. (*He moves over to a pleasant-looking middle-aged man*, TED.) Hullo, Ted. How goes it? Drink all right?

TED: Fine. Lovely to see you.

JOCK: Lovely to see you, believe me.

TED: I was just going to come and rescue you. Who's that dreadful harpy cornering you? I thought she was going to take a bite out of your Adam's apple.

JOCK: Oh, Susan something. One of the brightest, fearless, hard-hitting columnists in the business.

TED: Oh, *that*. . . . Feeling tired?

JOCK: How'd you guess?

TED: All that dubbing. Did she give you a fearful whack on the shoulder? Arise——

JOCK: I'll go to Innisfree, thank you. I'm a bit tired of knighthood gags.

TED: Sorry.

JOCK: I know it's funny, but you came.

TED: Sure. Sleeping?

JOCK: Pretty bad.

TED: Even that new lot I gave you?

JOCK: Bit worse if anything.

TED: We'll see if we can't think of something else. Can you come to see me?

JOCK: Bit difficult at present. I'm going to New York next week. Export Gala. All that.

TED: Then I'll drop in sometime. On my way home.

JOCK: That's good of you, Ted. You might look at the old woman too.

TED: Will you see your ex over there?

JOCK: I suppose so. It's the only way I can get to see the boy.

TED: How old is he?

JOCK: Fifteen. Long hair. All that.

TED: Yankee accent?

JOCK: Oh, God, yes.

TED: Better give you some calm-you-downers.

JOCK: Please. Ted, would you excuse me. I've just seen someone . . . I've not seen him for years.

TED: You go on, dear boy. Actually, I'm rather enjoying myself. Some pretty girls. . . .

JOCK: Well, watch it. I don't want you performing any abortions in my house. (*He moves over to a youngish-looking man in his forties.*) Stephen!

STEPHEN: Jock—well!

18

JOCK: But this is marvellous. I didn't know you were coming.

STEPHEN: Your wife came to my exhibition yesterday and asked me on the spot. I don't know whether she meant to.

JOCK: She didn't tell me. I can't get over seeing you here. Did she buy anything?

STEPHEN: I don't think so. But she seemed enthusiastic. And knows what she's talking about—which helps.

JOCK: I wish I did.

STEPHEN: You do pretty well. Anyway, here I am.

JOCK: Listen, could we have lunch or something one day?

STEPHEN: Love to. When?

JOCK: I can't hear in all this din. Could you ring me?

STEPHEN: Sure.

JOCK: And don't be put off by my secretary. She just tries to be stern and off-putting.

STEPHEN: Of course. I'll be persistent. I'll tell the truth—at school together.

JOCK: That doesn't sound very convincing. Just say you're the famous painter. That'll impress her. She's frightfully keen on art and galleries and things. Goes with her girl-friend. You won't believe this——

STEPHEN: What?

JOCK: I say you won't believe this but I had a dream about you the other day. Of course, it was you as a *boy*. But it's odd. After all this time.

(STEPHEN *smiles and raises his glass.*)

STEPHEN: Well—here we are.

JOCK: Yes.

STEPHEN: Congratulations. Nice party.

JOCK: Wish they'd all go. You and I could talk.

STEPHEN: We will. Your wife's beautiful.

JOCK: I do believe she's enjoying herself. . . . She *is* pretty.

STEPHEN: Well—here's to our meeting.

JOCK: Yes.

STEPHEN: Reunion sounds like old boys' dinners or regiments and things.

JOCK: Yes. Here's to it.

19

12. INT. MELLORS' SITTING ROOM NIGHT

Debris of party. Ashtrays, bottles, clutter etc. MARIO *is sluggishly and unwillingly clearing up.* JOCK *watches him.*

JOCK. I should leave it until the morning, Mario. It'll take you all night.

MARIO: Very good, sir. Sir Jock, I mean, sir. Good night, sir.

JOCK: 'Night.

(MARIO *goes out.* JOCK *looks wearily for a clean glass, cleans out a dirty one with his handkerchief and pours himself a drink. He sits down and looks round the room. Presently his* WIFE *calls from the hall. He grimaces and sticks out his tongue at the door.*)

LADY MELLOR (*V.O.*): Jock!

JOCK: Yes.

LADY MELLOR: What are you doing?

JOCK: Thinking. Sort of.

LADY MELLOR: Well, you can sort of do that in bed.

JOCK: Just coming.

LADY MELLOR: You're not having another drink, are you?

JOCK: No. Are you?

LADY MELLOR: Oh, please yourself. Only you're the one who's got a meeting and you know what you'll feel like.

JOCK: That's right . . . I think I do know.

(*Her footsteps are heard up the stairs. A door closes rather sharply. He takes another drink and stares in silence.*)

13. INT. MELLORS' BEDROOM NIGHT

They're both in bed. Pause.

JOCK: You didn't tell me you'd met Stephen.

LADY MELLOR: Didn't I?

JOCK: No. You didn't.

LADY MELLOR: Just forgot I suppose.

JOCK: Funny thing to forget.

LADY MELLOR: What's so funny about it?

JOCK: Oh, I don't know . . . I've talked about him so often to you.

LADY MELLOR: You talk about a lot of things. Or, at least, a *few* things a *lot*. . . . Anyway, you haven't seen him for twenty years or so.

JOCK: Exactly.

LADY MELLOR: You're always trying to double back down some bye-way.

JOCK: It's getting light.

LADY MELLOR: It doesn't work. . . . Try and sleep, Jock.

JOCK (*eyes wide open at the curtains*): Sure. 'Night. . . . 'Morning. . . .

LADY MELLOR: I feel frightful. And we've got to go to the bleeding opera.

JOCK: I'm sorry.

LADY MELLOR: What about? Feeling frightful or the opera?

JOCK: Both. Shall I cancel?

LADY MELLOR: Oh, no. *You* like it.

JOCK: You can dress up.

LADY MELLOR: Thanks. You mean sit in the hairdresser's all the afternoon.

JOCK: Well—that's life. Did you buy any? Of Stephen's pictures?

LADY MELLOR: No.

JOCK: Any good?

LADY MELLOR: Quite. Not dazzling.

JOCK: Who dazzles?

LADY MELLOR: One or two. Here and there.

JOCK: Now and then.

LADY MELLOR: I'm trying to sleep.

JOCK: Sorry. I'm glad you enjoyed yourself. . . .
(*She curls up, her back to him. He smokes a cigarette. It glows in the early light.*)

14. EXT. MELLORS' HOUSE DAY
The CHAUFFEUR *opens the door of his Bentley for him and* JOCK *gets in.*

15. EXT. LONDON STREETS MALL ETC. MOVING CAR DAY

JOCK *sits back watching the* TOURISTS *gaping with their cascading cameras outside Buckingham Palace.*

JOCK: London doesn't seem to belong to us any more, Tom.

TOM: No, sir. I know what you mean, sir.

JOCK: Look at it. London—To Let. Look at *them*.

TOM: Perfect nuisance if you ask me, sir. Block up the roads. Fill up the restaurants. . . . Still——

JOCK: Yes?

TOM: Well, I suppose we depend on *them*, sir.

JOCK: Depend?

TOM: Yes, sir, well if it weren't for their money, all their dollars and marks and things, we'd be even worse off than we are today.

JOCK: Yes. . . .

TOM: I mean *you'd* know more about all that than almost anyone, sir.

(*He peers up at the Hilton Hotel.*)

16. INT. MELLOR'S OFFICE   DAY

He is with his secretary.

JOCK: Have you booked my flight to New York?

SECRETARY: Not yet. But there's plenty of time, and I've warned the travel agent and made the usual arrangements.

JOCK: You've got the Covent Garden tickets?

SECRETARY: I'll give them to you before you go home.

JOCK: Somebody called Stephen Grain hasn't rung, has he?

SECRETARY: You mean the painter? No.

JOCK: Put him through if he does.

SECRETARY: Right.

JOCK: Nothing else?

SECRETARY: That seems to be all. Unless you've anything. There's the lunch at Grosvenor House.

JOCK: What's the topic of the day?

SECRETARY: Management and Manpower Planning.

JOCK: Ring Lord Thing and make my apologies.

SECRETARY: Yes, Sir Jock.

JOCK: What's the matter?

SECRETARY: Matter?

JOCK: You look disapproving.

SECRETARY: I just thought——

JOCK: It was important. Everybody does. I can't listen to that ignorant, ponderous, illiterate old shop steward going on about the heads of industry and the man on the shop floor. That's where they should have left *him*.

SECRETARY: Yes, Sir Jock.

JOCK: And I think we'll forget *that*. I'm beginning to feel like an upgraded toastmaster.

SECRETARY: Yes, sir.

JOCK: Oh, see if you can get Stephen Grain for me, will you? Now. Thanks.

(*She nods, goes out, he watches her. Then turns to look at the skyline. There is a buzz from the desk.*)

Yes.

SECRETARY (*V.O.*): There's no reply from Mr. Grain. Shall I try the Royal College?

JOCK: Er—no. I expect he'll ring. Get me Dr. Williams, will you? (*He waits.*) Ted? How are you? Good. . . . Well I'm glad someone enjoyed themselves. Look, sorry to bother you at work. . . . Could you manage lunch. . . ? Today? . . . Never mind. It doesn't matter. . . . Well, it's short notice. . . . No, nothing wrong. Just thought it would be nice to meet. No, nothing wrong. Really, everything's fine. . . . Well, when you can . . . 'bye. (*He puts the phone down, puts on his coat.*)

17. INT. OUTER OFFICE   DAY

SECRETARY *typing*. JOCK *enters*.

JOCK: I'm having lunch with Dr. Williams. I'll probably be late.

SECRETARY: Shall I book you a table?

JOCK: No thanks. I expect we'll take pot luck. See you. . . .

SECRETARY: You look very tired.

JOCK: Late night. Just another late night.

(*She watches him go.*)

23

18. EXT. ST. JAMES'S PARK   DAY
From a bench JOCK *watches children.* DUCKS. TOURISTS *particularly.*
Two of them sit beside him.
TOURIST: Beautiful day.
JOCK: Yes.
TOURIST: Just beautiful.
WIFE: Great. Do you *live* here?
JOCK: I do.
WIFE: We just love it.
TOURIST: Really. There are so many wonderful things to do,
    and see here.
JOCK: So they tell me. I believe that rain is forecast for later.
TOURIST: Is that so?
WIFE: Oh, dear. That's a *shame*.
JOCK: But I wouldn't rely on it. Good afternoon.
    (*He walks away. The* TOURISTS *seem puzzled by the whole*
    thing and then look at each other. The MALE *of the two*
    starts playing happily with his cine-camera.)

19. EXT. COVENT GARDEN   NIGHT
JOCK *and* LADY MELLOR *get out of the car assisted by* TOM.

20. INT. COVENT GARDEN CRUSH BAR   NIGHT
JOCK *and his* WIFE *are sipping champagne. He is looking at his*
programme.
JOCK: All right?
LADY MELLOR: O.K.
JOCK: What are you looking at?
LADY MELLOR: I'm not "looking at". I just wondered if there's
    anyone I know.
JOCK: Only too likely I'm afraid.
LADY MELLOR: Can you tell me what on earth this damn thing
    is about?
JOCK: I'm doing my best. Do you want to go?
LADY MELLOR: After getting into all this?
JOCK: Well, it says after the shipwreck, he's sold himself to

24

some god or other and then when he sees the girl, he declares his love in a thrilling aria.

LADY MELLOR: Girl?

JOCK: Then later on, the King, that's the one with the beard and ringlets, breaks into agitated fury.

LADY MELLOR: Oh, that's what he was doing. I thought he couldn't stand the woman.

JOCK: The young chap regrets his rash vow. . . . Then it says the King at first doesn't recognize his son . . . don't quite follow this. . . .

LADY MELLOR: I didn't think you were very clear.

JOCK: The act comes to a close with the King rushing out in extreme distress.

LADY MELLOR: Oh, God! How many more intervals?

JOCK: Two.

LADY MELLOR: Two!

JOCK: Look, I'm sorry, I didn't write the bloody thing. The music sounds pretty good to me, and at least it's better than all those pouves prancing about in white tights flashing their jock straps at that piss-elegant meat market.

LADY MELLOR: I'm afraid I don't agree. Why do you *enjoy* your ignorance so much? At least the ballet audience isn't so *square*. Look at those little numbers. They're *upholstered*.

JOCK: Oh, well, you can think about what you'll have for dinner.

LADY MELLOR: I'm on a diet.

JOCK: How exciting for you.

LADY MELLOR: *You* could do with one.

JOCK: For both of us.

LADY MELLOR: Take a look at yourself sometime. You look as if you've done too much childbearing.

JOCK: A little louder. They can't hear you on the balcony.

LADY MELLOR: Sorry. Your dignity.

JOCK: There's the bell. We'd better move.

LADY MELLOR: I haven't finished my drink.

(*He waits.*)

JOCK: Let's try to make a go of it. The evening. . . .

LADY MELLOR: I have. . . . For years. . . .

JOCK: Are you *very* unhappy?

LADY MELLOR: Work it out if you can—Sir Jock.

    (*She leaves him to follow her down the stairs.*)

21. INT. TRAVELLING CAR   NIGHT

JOCK *and his* WIFE *travel home in silence.*

22. EXT. MELLORS' HOUSE   NIGHT

They get out of the car.

JOCK: Good night, Tom.

TOM: Good night, Sir Jock. Good night, my lady.

    (*They go into the house.*)

23. INT. MELLORS' BEDROOM   NIGHT

LADY MELLOR *is removing her make-up. He is reading the evening newspaper in bed. Pause.*

LADY MELLOR: You enjoy these silences, don't you?

JOCK: What?

LADY MELLOR: Don't pretend you're deaf. . . . How long is this one going to last?

JOCK: There's not much to talk about is there? By now?

LADY MELLOR: Why isn't there? There *should* be.

JOCK: Should. Yes. Should.

    (*She goes over to him and sits on the bed.*)

LADY MELLOR: Well?

JOCK: Well?

LADY MELLOR: Is that all? Haven't you anything to say to me?

JOCK: I——

LADY MELLOR: Well?

JOCK: Suppose I *should*. But I haven't.

LADY MELLOR: I see.

JOCK: No. You don't. Nor I. Get to sleep. You're tired.

LADY MELLOR: Thanks.

JOCK: All right. Don't.

LADY MELLOR: Thanks again.

JOCK: It's a clear alternative.

LADY MELLOR: I hate you.

JOCK: I know.

LADY MELLOR: Then why don't you *do* something? Why don't you *do* something about it?

JOCK: I don't know . . . what? And if I did, I doubt I could do it.

LADY MELLOR: Well, thanks for another lovely evening.

JOCK: I'm sorry. We'll not go again.

LADY MELLOR: Threats?

JOCK: Whatever you please.

LADY MELLOR: God, you're a pompous man.

JOCK: Yes. I *am* a pompous man. It's expected of me.

LADY MELLOR: I can see you at board meetings.

JOCK: You could.

LADY MELLOR: You mean I should?

JOCK: Should. No. Not should. Well . . . it pays for the clothes on your back.

LADY MELLOR: Oh, thanks. . . .

JOCK: Vulgar——

LADY MELLOR: As ever.

JOCK: Indeed. But then *you*'ve had too many sleeping pills. Go to bed.

LADY MELLOR: Why?

JOCK: Then don't go to bed. You're free.

LADY MELLOR: Am I? What's free? Are *you* free?

JOCK: Ah!

LADY MELLOR: *Are* you? Are you free?

JOCK: No.

LADY MELLOR: There.

JOCK: There. There's a very dreary lot of people.

LADY MELLOR: *Are* a dreary lot of people.

JOCK: Are.

LADY MELLOR: Are you one of them?

JOCK: Not of this lot, actually.

LADY MELLOR: Actually.

JOCK: Yes. Don't think you can provoke me by now. I *could* smash your face in, but I don't intend to.

27

LADY MELLOR: Is that so? Really.

JOCK: Really. But don't push it.

LADY MELLOR: Is the poor old lion's tail whisking? Is it? Is it whisking?

JOCK: They're called The Trobriand Islanders.

LADY MELLOR: Who? The mangy old lions?

JOCK: No. Those very dull people who are always cropping up all over the place. To prove some clear——

LADY MELLOR: What?

JOCK: Obvious point.

LADY MELLOR: Why don't you kiss me?

JOCK: Because—simply—you no longer care for it.

LADY MELLOR: No?

JOCK: No.

LADY MELLOR: Poor Mr. Chairman.

JOCK: They. . . .

LADY MELLOR: Who?

JOCK: The Trobriand Islanders.

LADY MELLOR: Oh, yes. What about them?

JOCK: They have—among other things. . . .

LADY MELLOR: Other things?

JOCK: Other things. No word for "why" or "because". . . .

LADY MELLOR: Fascinating.

JOCK: Do go to bed.

LADY MELLOR: Why?

JOCK: On the other hand——

LADY MELLOR: Oh—Mr. Chairman.

JOCK: Don't.

LADY MELLOR: Sir Jock!

JOCK: Well?

LADY MELLOR: I *can't* resist that.

JOCK: I thought not.

LADY MELLOR: I'm coming . . . I'm coming to bed.

(*She gets up, goes round the bed, gets in, smiles at him with sleepy malice and turning her bedside light out, goes to sleep almost immediately, her back to him. He watches her and closes his eyes.*)

24. INT. MELLORS' BEDROOM   NIGHT
*He lies awake, looking at partially opened light from the curtain.
She is sleeping. He gets up slowly, seeking out his dressing-gown
and slippers, intent on silence, and, with the same middle of night
concentration, opens the bedroom door noiselessly and goes out.*

25. INT. MELLORS' HOUSE   LANDING   NIGHT
JOCK *pauses outside a door. Then goes in.*

26. INT. MYRA'S BEDROOM   NIGHT
JOCK *feels his way towards the bed. He carefully pulls the curtains
a little and some light falls on* MYRA's *face asleep in bed. He sits and
watches her sleeping. He looks around the room. Presently the door
opens and* LADY MELLOR *appears. He moves swiftly so as not to
disturb the child, who moves, and goes out past his wife.*

27. INT. MELLORS' SITTING-ROOM   NIGHT
Both are in dressing-gowns. He is getting himself a drink.
LADY MELLOR: What are you doing?
JOCK: Having a drink. Want one?
LADY MELLOR: No. I mean up there.
JOCK: Just looking.
LADY MELLOR: Looking?
JOCK: Why don't you go back to bed?
LADY MELLOR: You want to get away from me.
JOCK: Sort of.
LADY MELLOR: Why do you want to reproduce yourself?
JOCK: I don't. Believe me.
LADY MELLOR: You did.
JOCK: No more.
LADY MELLOR: Well—you *have*.
JOCK: Have I?
LADY MELLOR: Haven't you?
JOCK: No. I would say not.
LADY MELLOR: "I would say not." *I* had to *have* her. . . . Not
   you.

29

JOCK: Right.

LADY MELLOR: Right.

JOCK: Well——

LADY MELLOR: Well, what?

JOCK: We were mistaken.

LADY MELLOR: *You* were mistaken. I always *knew*.

JOCK: You always do. . . .

LADY MELLOR: You're bored with me, aren't you?

JOCK: Yes.

LADY MELLOR: How much?

JOCK: Enough.

LADY MELLOR: *Thank* you, Daddy.

JOCK: Drink?

LADY MELLOR: How bored do you think I am with you?

JOCK: More.

LADY MELLOR: Right.

JOCK: And longer.

LADY MELLOR: Damn right.

(They sit in silence.)

JOCK: Why don't you go to bed?

LADY MELLOR: Why should I? It's *my* house.

JOCK: True. You're half asleep. That's all.

LADY MELLOR: But only half. . . . Why are you bored?

JOCK: I don't know. God, you're like that journalist.

LADY MELLOR: But you are. . . .

JOCK: I read somewhere. . . .

LADY MELLOR: What?

JOCK: I believe that Arthur Balfour. . . .

LADY MELLOR: Who?

JOCK: Balfour. Arthur. British Statesman and Prime Minister.

LADY MELLOR: What *are* you talking about? I think you're
      going mad.

JOCK: So do I.

LADY MELLOR: What about him?

JOCK: Who? Oh! I believe he used to go——

LADY MELLOR: Go where?

JOCK: Go pale. With boredom. He used to go *pale* with boredom.

LADY MELLOR: Poor old thing. . . . Poor old Arthur.

JOCK: Yes. That's what I thought. . . .

LADY MELLOR: You don't care about that child at all, do you?

JOCK: Um?

LADY MELLOR: *Do* you?

JOCK: I'm sure you're right.

LADY MELLOR: *I'm* right.

JOCK: Do you want to go back to bed?

LADY MELLOR: Why not? Let's have fun.

JOCK: That's right.

LADY MELLOR: Let's.

JOCK: Let's.

(*She turns sleepily up the stairs.*)

I'll turn out the lights.

28. INT. MELLORS' BATHROOM   DAY

JOCK *is in his pyjamas shaving with electric razor. He looks down at it and watches himself shave as it whirrs away on his chin.*

JOCK (*V.O.*): Good old West Germany.

The razor that really cares for you. Discretion. Efficiency. Beauty. Simplicity. Superb. Untouched by Human Mind. More or less. Leadership. Co-operation.

Shave yourself. Oh shave yourself, it's later than you think. . . . Your head. . . . Armpits. No place in today's fast-moving, fast-thinking world for hairy armpits. . . . Get ahead with a shave. If you can't have a shave, have a—my own Lille Marlene . . . my own Lille Marlene.

29. INT. MELLORS' BEDROOM   DAY

He is now fully dressed and looks down at his wife. She looks up sleepily.

JOCK: 'Bye.

LADY MELLOR: 'Bye.

30. EXT. SMALL AIRFIELD   DAY

JOCK *gets into small* PRIVATE PLANE. *The* PILOT *smiles cheerily and they start to take off.*

31. INT. PLANE   DAY

JOCK *looks out at the landscape below. The* PILOT *is beside him,
smoking.*

PILOT: Still looks quite good.

JOCK: What's that?

PILOT: I say the old place still looks pretty good. Down *there.*

JOCK: Oh. Yes. Not bad. (*He nods and turns to look away.*)

32. INT. CONFERENCE ROOM   DAY

JOCK *is seated on the platform. The* CHAIRMAN *of the meeting is
introducing him to the assembled audience.*

CHAIRMAN: . . . which is why if we are to survive in this fast-
moving fast-thinking world today, we must constantly be
one move ahead or lose our place in an ever-expanding and
changing world . . .

(JOCK *looks down at his brief-case. Then at a* GIRL *farther
down the row. She returns his stare coolly and he looks
away.*)

33. INT. CONFERENCE ROOM   DAY

JOCK *is on his feet at the microphone, having been introduced by the*
CHAIRMAN. *The applause dies away.*

JOCK: Mr. Chairman. Gentlemen. Excuse me, *Ladies* and
Gentlemen. As our Chairman says, in this fast-moving
world, no one can move faster than the ladies. Let's not
forget it . . .

(THE GIRL *at the end of the row can't even bring herself to
smile at the self-mocking glibness of it. She just closes her
eyes and waits for him to go on.*)

34. EXT. FACTORY   DAY

TOM *is waiting with the car for* JOCK. *The empty forecourt of the
factory is suddenly filled with workers—some collecting their cars,
a few on motor bikes, some walking. A few give* TOM *a cold eye.
Aware of all this, and used to it, he adopts the chauffeur remoteness
of a guardsman outside a Royal Palace.* JOCK *appears, takes in the
emptying factory, and heads for the haven of the car.*

JOCK: Thank you, Tom.

35. INT. CAR DAY

JOCK *watches through the window as the crowds block the progress of the car.*

TOM: Come *on*!

(*A face turns and grins.*)

JOCK: I think we chose a bad time?

TOM: What's that, Sir Jock?

JOCK: They don't like us.

TOM: I don't know why they have to walk like that. What's that, sir?

JOCK: Why should they? Neither do I? And why should I? I *know* them. I'm one of them. They don't know me. And—what's more—they never will. Don't honk the horn, Tom. They'll strike soon enough.

(*They proceed slowly through the crowd.* JOCK *huddles back into his seat. He looks at a paper but gives up.*)

36. EXT. ROAD DAY

The car finally makes its way out of the factory gates, then, losing the main body of the crowd, speeds on its way.

37. INT. MELLORS' BEDROOM NIGHT

JOCK *enters. He turns on a small light by the bedside.* LADY MELLOR *is in bed asleep. She stirs, moans then suddenly sits up.*

LADY MELLOR: Oh—it's you.

JOCK: I'm sorry. I didn't mean to wake you.

LADY MELLOR: Oh. . . . What time is it?

JOCK: About one.

LADY MELLOR: Have you eaten?

JOCK: Yes. Do go back to sleep.

(*He takes off his jacket and begins to undress. She watches him.*)

JOCK: Please—go back to sleep.

LADY MELLOR: How was it?

JOCK: How was what?

33

LADY MELLOR: British Industry and the Future? The World. All that. . . .

JOCK: The same. Adjusting itself. . . . Dynamic.

LADY MELLOR: Jolly good. Were you dynamic?

JOCK: Fairly.

LADY MELLOR: Jolly good. . . . Well?

JOCK: Well?

LADY MELLOR: What else did you do?

JOCK: Oh—sit in directors' aeroplanes . . . cars.

LADY MELLOR: Talked to Tom?

JOCK: Talked to Tom.

LADY MELLOR: Do you know what?

JOCK: No. What?

LADY MELLOR: You've got no friends.

JOCK: Yes.

LADY MELLOR: What's that?

JOCK: I said "Yes".

LADY MELLOR: You're forty-seven and a bit and you've got no friends.

JOCK: Well. . . .

LADY MELLOR: What? I can't hear you. . . .

JOCK: I was aware of it.

LADY MELLOR: Oh, you were? Were aware. Were you. Oh, good. (*Pause.*) What's the matter? Why don't you say something?

JOCK: I think I've——

LADY MELLOR: What?

JOCK: Said it. Said it all.

LADY MELLOR: Really?

JOCK: Can I get you something?

LADY MELLOR: No. . . . *Why* do you think you've got no friends?

JOCK: Perhaps because——

LADY MELLOR: What?

JOCK: Oh—I'm not very likeable.

LADY MELLOR: What else?

JOCK: It could be——

34

LADY MELLOR: It could be—do tell me.

JOCK: It's not an age for friendship.

LADY MELLOR: I see. You missed out.

    (JOCK *starts to dress again.*)

    What are you doing? Are you leaving?

JOCK: Yes.

LADY MELLOR: Me?

JOCK: Yes.

LADY MELLOR: I see. . . . You're frightened, aren't you?

JOCK: Yes . . . I am.

LADY MELLOR: What of? Me?

JOCK: A little.

LADY MELLOR: The Big World?

JOCK: A little.

LADY MELLOR: Well—if you go, you won't come back, will
    you? Promise?

JOCK: Sure.

LADY MELLOR: Good. Because, you know what, nobody needs *you.*

JOCK: That's something.

LADY MELLOR: Sir Jock Something. . . . Who wants you?

JOCK: No one.

LADY MELLOR: Right. Good night. Leave your door key.

JOCK: I'll send it. Good night.

    (*She turns out the light. She is asleep.*)

38. INT. CAR MOTORWAY   NIGHT

JOCK *is at the wheel. He drives, alert but absorbed in his thoughts.
Suddenly a car appears in his rear view mirror, yapping at his heels,
flashing its lights. Surprised, his reactions are slow and the flashing
and car-yapping become frantic. Finally, he pulls over to the side of
the road, and a jeering voice and waving arm from the other car
leave him behind to draw up. He comes to a stop and leans against
the wheel.*

39. INT. CAR   NIGHT

A light flashes on JOCK's *face. He looks up to see a* POLICEMAN *at
the window.*

40. INT. CAR   NIGHT

The POLICEMAN *is handing* JOCK *back his license.*

POLICEMAN: Well, I know there are a lot of inconsiderate folk around. But still—I wouldn't advise going to sleep at the roadside.

JOCK: No. Well. Thank you.

POLICEMAN: Good-bye, sir. Drive carefully then. . . .

(JOCK *looks at him, nods and moves off, watched by the* POLICEMAN *and the* DRIVER *of the* POLICE CAR.)

41. INT. STEPHEN GRAIN'S STUDIO   DAY

Victorian, lofty but cosy. JOCK *stares at one of* STEPHEN'*s rather romantic nudes while the painter makes some coffee on a little oil stove.*

JOCK: She kept saying, "I'm lonely . . . I'm so lonely. . . ." Then she went to sleep. Which is lucky. . . .

STEPHEN: Is she?

JOCK: What?

STEPHEN: Lonely.

JOCK: Oh, yes. Very.

STEPHEN: Are you?

JOCK: I suppose so. I don't think I'm even aware of it by this time.

STEPHEN: You equate it with courage?

JOCK: I dare say.

STEPHEN: It comes easy to some. Then it's no virtue. I mean, to me, for instance. But then I'm very selfish.

JOCK: Are you?

STEPHEN: Yes.

JOCK: Really?

STEPHEN: Not on a big scale. I don't involve people's lives. At least, I don't think I do. I've just marked out my own small area and I run it the way I want. I run a small, medium, private life. I've tried not to waste anything. I've got the modest public success I suppose I deserve. Difficult enough—but there. Strange for someone like you——

36

JOCK: What?

STEPHEN: To spread his investment so wide. Here. (*Hands him coffee.*) Why not a little brandy in it?

JOCK: Why not? Thanks.

STEPHEN: Don't be silly.

JOCK: At this time of the day. After so long. I felt I must see you—at that dreadful party. It's about thirty years, isn't it?

STEPHEN: I suppose it is. . . . There's no going back though, is there? *As* they say.

JOCK: No.

STEPHEN: What about going forward?

JOCK: Well?

STEPHEN: I thought all you chaps were all beavering away at that. You'll all be dead, anyway.

JOCK: Or mad.

STEPHEN: What are you going to do? I mean, leave home?

JOCK: Oh, I suppose so. I have to go to New York next week.

STEPHEN: *Have* to?

JOCK: Well, I'm going. In the meantime—I, oh, I think I'll go and see my father. He's pretty old. . . . And my sister. She's married to some high-flying academic at Cambridge.

STEPHEN: And in New York?

JOCK: I'll see my son. And my ex-wife. Have to do *that*.

STEPHEN: And the meantime?

JOCK: Oh—think I'll look up my doctor. Driving on motorways doesn't really agree with me. I'm sorry I descended on you in this way.

STEPHEN: It's all right. I never start work before ten-thirty or so. More coffee?

JOCK: No. I must go. (*At nude.*) Is it for sale?

STEPHEN: When it's finished.

JOCK: She reminds me.

STEPHEN: I wonder if you remind *her*!

JOCK: I'm sure not. Still—where would she be?

STEPHEN: In your remembrance. I wouldn't look anywhere else,
  if I were you.
JOCK: No. Still . . . I do like it. Very much. She's hard to
  escape.
STEPHEN: You shall have it. If you still want it later.
  (*They look at the nude together.*)

42. EXT. STEPHEN'S STUDIO   STREET   DAY
A large group of young men are coolly and systematically kicking
JOCK's *car with the clear object of doing as much damage as possible.*
STEPHEN *and* JOCK *advance towards them. The young men—and a*
few girls—stop almost absent-mindedly and move off.
STEPHEN: They're from the college, I'm afraid. . . . I *teach*
  them.
JOCK: I see.
STEPHEN: You see—to them—you're——
JOCK: The enemy.
STEPHEN: Not much one can do about it. Is there much damage?
JOCK: Nothing new.
  (STEPHEN *opens the door for him. He gets into the driver's*
  seat of his near-wrecked car.)
STEPHEN: Try not to feel too badly.
JOCK: About what?
STEPHEN: Oh—anything.
JOCK: No. But I will. I do.
STEPHEN: Well——
JOCK: Thank you, Stephen. You've been patient.
STEPHEN: It comes—easily.
JOCK: We never discussed school.
STEPHEN: We're the only products.
JOCK: Yes. The only products. 'Bye.
STEPHEN: 'Bye. I'll send you the picture.
JOCK: Thanks. (JOCK *drives off in his battered car.*)

43. INT. TED WILLIAMS'S SURGERY, HARLEY STREET   DAY
He is taking JOCK's *blood pressure, who watches him pump the*
  bulb.

JOCK: I always think you're going to blow up my arm.

TED: You should know better than that by now.

JOCK: Like those, oh, demolition experts.

TED: I'm not really in the demolition business.

JOCK: No. Would you be—a Preservationist?

TED: That's all we are.

JOCK: Yes. Well, there has to be a *name* for it, doesn't there?

TED: What's the matter, Jock?

JOCK: I'm here to find out.

TED: *All* bad is it?

JOCK: Yes. I would say so. Pretty. Wouldn't you?

TED: Fairly. I suppose.

JOCK: Do *you* have—friends?

TED: Not what I think you mean. Otherwise—some.

JOCK: She looked at me with such contempt.

TED: Who did?

JOCK: The girl on the platform. When I was speaking. So-called speaking. With *such* genuine dislike. Cool dislike. Quite exciting.

TED: Sounds it.

JOCK: Oh—up to a point. I resented it as well. She has no right to, well, be sure of herself and me and judge and look, look at me like that. However.

TED: However?

JOCK: However, she did. Do you want me checked up?

TED: Why not?

JOCK: I thought so. Well—when I come back from New York.

TED: What's it for——

JOCK: Selling. Us. Selling *Us*.

TED: Well, I hope you get a good price.

JOCK: Can't guarantee it, dear boy. You may be the best but they may not want you. What are you writing out there? Something special?

TED: No. But useful.

JOCK: Thanks. It'll help with all the grinning airlines.

TED: It should. So—when you come back. Where are you going now?

JOCK: Oh, I'll drop in on my father. Just to make sure he's in an upright position. He won't know if I'm there or not.
TED: Is he all right?
JOCK: Good for years. We simply don't have much well, much, *no* feeling for one another.
TED: Why go and see him?
JOCK: Just to look. Afterwards, I shall go and *look* at my sister.
TED (*looks out into street*): They *did* make a mess of your car, my God!
OCK: Yes. Quite a good job, I thought. Can I put my clothes on?
TED: Of course.

44. INT. FATHER'S FLAT   NIGHT

JOCK'S FATHER *is about eighty, sharp but not interested in anything much outside a few feet radius of himself. That is, his dog,* SAM—*at his feet—and the television set, which flickers soundlessly across the room. The old man finds it hard to take his eyes off the set—to* JOCK'*s irritation. Both bored with one another.*

FATHER: Well. . . .
JOCK: Well, what?
FATHER: What?
JOCK: You were going to say something.
FATHER: Oh, was I? Well. . . .
JOCK: Do you want me to turn that on?
FATHER: Um?
JOCK: Shall I turn it *on* for you?
FATHER: Oh, no thanks. Nothing on yet.
JOCK: Oh I see.
FATHER: There's Treble Your Stake.
JOCK: What's that like?
FATHER: But that's not on till quarter past.
JOCK: Good, is it?
FATHER: There's the News just before that. Old Sam likes that, don't you, boy?
JOCK: I'll bet. Got to keep up with the News.
FATHER: What?

JOCK: With the news.

FATHER: I never watch it. Too depressing . . . I've seen *you*
once or twice.

JOCK: What in?

FATHER: Can't remember it now. Made you look old I thought.

JOCK: I expect I felt old.

FATHER: That's what they said next door.

JOCK: Well, *you're* looking young.

FATHER: Young? I feel it. I suppose you *are* getting on a bit.
You must expect a difference.

JOCK: A difference?

FATHER: Yes. Old Sam's not the same.

JOCK: He looks the same. Smells the same.
(FATHER *doesn't get this at all.*)

FATHER: Well, I look after him, don't I? Go walkies, don't we,
eh? Twice a day. Go walkies. Then I cook all his food in
the morning. Right after breakfast. Won't eat anything
uncooked. Rabbit mostly.

JOCK: Yes, you told me.

FATHER: Nothing uncooked, will you, old devil?

JOCK: So—you're all right then?

FATHER: Me? Oh, I'm all right.

JOCK: Nothing I can do?

FATHER: No thank you, son. You look after me very well. And
the people next door are very good.

JOCK: Yes. Only I'm going away to New York.

FATHER: Oh, yes?

JOCK: America.

FATHER: America. Dreadful place. Saw a thing on the other
night about it. Killing and shooting one another.

JOCK: Yes. I'm not exactly keen to go.

FATHER: I wouldn't like to go to a place like that. . . . (*Pause.*)
Are you going to see the boy?

JOCK: I expect so.

FATHER: Pity you don't see him more often.

JOCK: Yes. It's a difficult situation.

FATHER: He never comes to see *me*. I haven't seen him, oh, not

D  41

for years.

JOCK: He lives in America, Father.

FATHER: Wouldn't like a child of mine growing up there.

JOCK: I didn't have much choice.

FATHER: You what?

JOCK: Anyway, he's more or less grown up. . . .

(*Pause.*)

FATHER: Will you see *her*?

JOCK: I expect it will be obligatory . . . yes, I shall.

FATHER: Never liked her much.

JOCK: I know. You've said.

FATHER: I shouldn't say so of course.

JOCK: No.

FATHER: Thought a lot of her chances, that one.

JOCK: Some of them have come off.

FATHER: Ambitious. Ambitious woman. Your mother wasn't like that.

JOCK: I'd better be going.

FATHER: What—already? I don't see you very often. How's the *little* one?

JOCK: Myra's fine. They're both fine.

FATHER: Give them my love. And thanks for the bottle. You're a good boy. . . . And tell your sister to come and see me sometimes.

JOCK: I will.

FATHER: Of course, *he's* a big chap at Cambridge.

JOCK: I *do* know.

FATHER: What's the matter? Are you in a hurry or something?

JOCK: Don't get up. I'll let myself out.

FATHER: Oh, are you going? I won't get up. Could you turn the sound up?

JOCK: Of course. Sam must see the News. Good night, Dad.

(*Kisses him on the forehead.*)

FATHER: Good-bye, son. Be careful over *there*.

(JOCK *pats his head.*)

Dreadful place.

(JOCK *pats the dog on the head.*)

JOCK: 'Bye, Sam.
> (*He goes out, leaving his* FATHER *and* SAM *watching the news in the little flickering room.*)

45. EXT. KINGS COLLEGE CAMBRIDGE   DAY
JOCK *is walking with his sister,* JAN. *She is younger than he is, quick, a little impatient, particularly with him.*
JOCK: God, it's cold.
JAN: Give me your arm then.
> (*He does.*)
JOCK: Talk about icy wind. I can see why Cromwell was like he was.
JAN: He wasn't a puffed up, protected business man.
JOCK: I don't feel very protected. Puffed up maybe.
JAN: Are you looking forward to New York?
JOCK: No.
JAN: Why go then?
JOCK: I've said I will. . . .
JAN: I don't understand you people.
JOCK: I'm not "you people". I'm your brother.
JAN: Sorry.
JOCK: No. I *am* "you people".
JAN: How's the old boy then?
JOCK: No different. I don't know why I ever expect he should be.
JAN: The funny thing is *you* don't really want change.
JOCK: Spare me a run-down on myself. I *do* know the area a little better than you.
JAN: Do you?
JOCK: Listen, I didn't come here for a little academic assessment.
JAN (*pause*): *Why* did you?
JOCK: I don't know.
> (*They stop.*)
> Looking at you. Listening to you, I *don't* know.
> (*They walk on.*)
> I *should* stop thumbing my way. . . .
JAN: I think perhaps you should. It's a national neurosis.

43

JOCK: I should have known you'd have a phrase for it.

JAN: You have quite a few of your own—even if they're all pretty third hand. I'm always reading them.

JOCK: You're quite right.

JAN: I'm sorry——

JOCK: No. You *are* . . . I've never been to Huntingdon.

JAN: What?

JOCK: That's Cromwell country, isn't it? I don't feel I'll somehow go now.

JAN: Well, Cromwell never went to New York. Cheer up.

JOCK: No. He never did. It does look good.

(*She glances at the buildings.*)

JAN: They want to pull the lot down. Put up a memorial to Ho Chi Minh or something in its place.

JOCK: Oh yes. I suppose so.

JAN: Well—why not? Maybe they're right.

JOCK: You live here. You should know.

JAN: We *all* live here. And we've got to go on getting used to it. Not just a few of us. What are you going to do?

JOCK: People keep asking me, "What am I going to do." A little less each day I should think. I've *done* enough. I should *stop*. Let's go in, shall we?

JAN: What?

JOCK: Inside. While it's still there.

JAN: Oh, all right. . . .

(*They go into the Chapel.*)

46. INT. AIRCRAFT DAY

JOCK *is settling, or trying to, into his seat. The* AIR HOSTESS, *radiating international safety regulation smugness, stands ready to do her pantomime. He stares at her with practised dislike. Looking around for an ally, he sees only a rather bossy* ATLANTIC COMMUTER *arranging his jacket neatly on the seat beside him. The* VOICE *on the tannoy system crackles away.*

V.O.: "And on behalf of Captain Lewis and his crew, we welcome you aboard."

JOCK: When do we get a *drink*?

44

(*The* ATLANTIC COMMUTER *and* AIR HOSTESS *glance at him and both turn away*.)

V.O.: I'm afraid there's a slight queue—er—here—at the runway. . . .

JOCK: Really? What a surprise.

V.O.: —and—er—in the meantime——

JOCK: Yes?

V.O.: There *will* be some delay before take off.

JOCK: Good heavens——

V.O.: While we take our place in the—er——

JOCK: Queue?

V.O.: Our estimated flying time to New York will be——

JOCK: Forever and ever, Amen. . . .

47. INT. AIRCRAFT   DAY

JOCK *looks down at the plastic food laid down before him by the* AIR HOSTESS. *He makes an effort with it, then tries to get rid of it but she is gone. The* COMMUTER *is tucking into his shrimp cocktail.*

COMMUTER: Do this often?

JOCK: It seems like it.

COMMUTER: What? D'you like New York?

JOCK: No.

COMMUTER: What?

JOCK: No.

COMMUTER: Oh. Why?

JOCK: I don't know. I just hope they, whoever that, they might have the privilege—drop a bomb on it.

COMMUTER: I hope it doesn't—happen while you're there.

JOCK: It could.

48. EXT. KENNEDY AIRPORT   DAY

JOCK *enters a group of squalid buildings leading to Health, Immigration Control and all that. An anxious* AIRLINE OFFICIAL *approaches.*

AIRLINE OFFICIAL: Sir Jock Mellor? Sir?

JOCK: No.

AIRLINE OFFICIAL: Oh.

JOCK: Sorry.

AIRLINE OFFICIAL: Only . . . Only, we have this Press Interview all
lined up here and——
JOCK: I think he's still on the plane.
AIRLINE OFFICIAL (*quite aware of the lie, but baffled*): Oh?
JOCK: He's probably thanking the Captain and his crew for
having him.
AIRLINE OFFICIAL: Yes. I see. Well——
JOCK: Excuse me. (*Moves on.*)
AIRLINE OFFICIAL: Excuse *me*.

49. INT. HEALTH CONTROL   DAY
HEALTH OFFICIAL: Can you tell me where you've been in the
past two weeks?
JOCK: London. Chipping Sodbury. And Cambridge.
HEALTH OFFICIAL: Chipping?
JOCK: Sodbury.
HEALTH OFFICIAL: And Cambridge. . . .
JOCK: England.

50. INT. CUSTOMS COUNTER   DAY
CUSTOMS OFFICER: Are these yours?
JOCK: Yes—I'll open them.
(*He does so and watches the* CUSTOMS OFFICER's *laborious
inspection. The* OFFICER *takes a book out of his suitcase and
appears to be actually reading it.*)
JOCK: It's the New Testament. . . . The King James Version.
CUSTOMS OFFICER: I know. . . .
(*He goes on looking.*)

51. INT. NEW YORK CAB   DAY
JOCK *sinks into the back as the cab leaves the* AIRPORT. *He stares at
the face of the* CAB DRIVER's *license. Then warily at the* DRIVER *at
the wheel. He slumps back even farther.*
JOCK (*V.O.*): No—I can't have one of those. They *invent* them.
I'll pretend to sleep. That won't stop him blowing his
filthy cigar smoke back at me.
DRIVER: Good trip?
JOCK (*V.O.*): Oh, no.

DRIVER: You came B.O.A.C.?

JOCK: Awful.

DRIVER: That so? You English?

JOCK: No.

DRIVER: Oh.

>   (*Pause*.)

>   Well—you *sound* English.

JOCK: Yes?

DRIVER: Where you from then?

JOCK: Penang.

DRIVER: Penang? Where's that?

JOCK: I hope your cigar chokes you to death.

DRIVER: What you say?

JOCK: Malaysia. Very good cigars. . . .

52. INT. HOTEL ROOM   DAY

JOCK's SON *is seated opposite him in silence. He is about sixteen, good looking, long haired.* JOCK *is looking out of the window at the glum-looking car-parking lot.*

JOCK: I haven't really bothered to even go out in the street this time.

SON (*politely*): No?

JOCK: There seems less and less point. Still, I suppose there are places to go if you live here.

SON: Sure.

JOCK: I think *I'll* have a drink.

SON: Go ahead.

JOCK: I'm sorry they wouldn't let you up.

SON: Who cares?

JOCK: I might not have seen you.

SON: Well—Mum turned up and put them right.

JOCK: I'd better go down and see her.

SON: I've got to be somewhere. . . .

JOCK: Let me know what you think about coming for a holiday.

SON: Right.

JOCK: I think you'd enjoy it.

SON: Sounds great.

47

(*They are both longing to disengage.*)

JOCK: There are so many places *I've* never been to either. After all—you're English too.

SON: So they tell me.

JOCK: Well—I may see you before I go. Or not. I've got to make a call. I expect your mother's still in the bar. Would you tell her I'll be down in five minutes?

SON: See you.

JOCK: Yes. I dare say. If not—you might still come over.

SON: Sure.

JOCK: 'Bye then.

(SON *nods amiably as* JOCK *picks up the telephone. He goes out.* JOCK *puts the receiver down. He looks at his watch.*)

53. INT. HOTEL LOBBY   DAY

JOCK'*s ex-wife,* BARBARA, *greets him. Rather over-friendly, so he is recoiling almost at once.*

JOCK: Sorry. Call, I'm afraid.

BARBARA: That's all right.

(*He kisses her quickly.*)

He was excited to see you.

JOCK: Was he? I've no idea.

BARBARA: Of course.

JOCK: Drink?

BARBARA: No, thanks.

JOCK: No, of course. Mustn't muddle the brain.

BARBARA: How long are you here?

JOCK: As short as possible.

BARBARA: Is it——

JOCK: I just want to get back.

BARBARA: If you want to see him again——

JOCK: No. Not here, anyway. I don't know how you work here —in this place.

BARBARA: It's not—cosy. But then where is? If that's what you might want.

JOCK: How's the big magazine business?

BARBARA: Selling. How's Industry? The old British kind, I mean?

48

JOCK: Trying.

BARBARA: So I read.

JOCK: Non-bleeding stop. Look, shall we have a truce and that drink?

BARBARA: Let's.

JOCK: Waiter.

I met Stephen Grain the other day.

BARBARA: The painter? You knew at school?

JOCK: That's right.

BARBARA: You were always talking about him. How was it?

JOCK: All right. No—I don't think we got on very well. No. . . .
I'm starting to worry if I'll get the plane back. . . . I
can't come here again.

BARBARA: I'm sorry.

JOCK: There's really nowhere left to *go*. Except for all the
places I've never been to.

BARBARA: You don't know what I feel each time I see you——

JOCK: No—well, we've only got five, ten minutes. I've got to go.

BARBARA: O.K.

JOCK: Tell me about the work.

(*The* WAITER *appears.*)

What will you have?

(*She looks at him slowly, gets up and goes.*)

A whisky sour.

WAITER: And the lady?

JOCK: *One* whisky sour. (*He stares at the busy lobby, piled with
arriving and departing suitcases.*)

54. INT. INTERNATIONAL TRADE CONFERENCE CONVENTION OF
LARGE HOTEL OF U.S. SWIMMING BATH TYPE   DAY
Everyone, including JOCK, *is listening to the* AFTER-LUNCH SPEAKER.
Apart from JOCK, *he is the* STAR SPEAKER *in all this smoke-filled big
business uneasiness. Minorish public school, also recently gonged
for his services to International trade—mostly wind, accountancy
and sharp lawyers—he takes his U.S. Convention course between
Burlington Arcade patronage and clear fawning on his acknow-
ledged betters.*

JOCK *stares at him and his listeners.*

STAR SPEAKER: . . . We all, or, at least, some of us remember, remarks about some of us here today, er—losing a role and not finding a new one. Well, before we go on to all the technical discussions—which is why we are all here—I would just like to say, say that that role is no longer necessary. It is forgotten. Forgotten with Special Relationships and all the rest of it. . . .

(*Some applause. Not much.*)

We are all, all of us in the world today, engaged in the same pursuit. That is, of making our way, and making our way triumphantly into the twenty-first century. Now—I won't keep you long because I know you're here and I'm here to listen to Jock Mellor talk about that very thing. But I feel I must make some sort of—not apology—but reference to certain inferences, particularly, I regret to say, in my own country—to er, to the implication that what are thought to be the unpleasant aspects of modern techniques and technology are due to some lack of "control". It is not *we* who are at fault in these matters. If anything, it is society itself. All these modern techniques are sophisticated exercises in compromise. It is up to society to decide what that compromise may or may not be. You cannot, repeat cannot, enjoy the joys of the modern jet engine, and they *are* the joys of speed and convenience, and whine about quietness and amenity.

(*Applause. More sustained this time.*)

Without these things, the things we, we here, set out to provide in these days of cost effective analysis. The great mass of human kind would continue to be deprived of those things that were once the privilege of a fortunate few. We can't go back to some programmed modern stone age. . . .

(*He sits down to applause.* JOCK *rises. . . .*)

JOCK: Gentlemen . . . I wish I could reply, no not reply, animadverte on is probably more adequate—on—my colleague's speech. He is, as you know, a highly

distinguished representative of my country here. We have
both been absorbed in our separate industries—and
common technologies—for, for something of a lifetime.
Trying to improve more, produce more, more what some
of us once called, what was it—quality of life? I think that
was it. Not *much* worse than "cost effective analysis". Or
"The joys of speed and convenience". Or "Programmed
Modern Stone Age" should last for a week or two. I
started out thinking one thing and now I agree with the
Speaker that technique *is* compromise. No doubt it's
inescapable. Still it would be nice to think, one didn't have
to go through all this toadying business to—avoid the
fact. . . .

v.o.: Sit down.

JOCK: No, sir. I will not sit down. I am your *invited* speaker.
You may leave if you wish.

v.o.: Sit. Down.

JOCK: So, I will read—as well as I can—my speech, which is
only slightly better than my predecessor's.

v.o.: Go home!

JOCK: I look forward to that. Somewhat. So, knowing how
really well we like each other. . . .

v.o.: Sit down.

JOCK: In this slum you have made into a desert—I'll read this—
speech. No. No. I don't think I will . . . I haven't the. . . .
(*He sits down. Then—gets up and goes out.*)

55. INT. HOTEL BEDROOM NEW YORK   NIGHT
JOCK *is on the telephone.*

JOCK: Hello—— No, *I'm* New York. I want London . . . Ted?
Hello. . . . Look—— Look, I'm just leaving this place. . . .
Yes. Look, I thought I might have those tests or whatever.
Can you lay it on for when I get back? Well, it might be a
good thing to lie low for a day or two . . . I think you'll
see. Thanks, Ted. Must go. (*As he replaces the receiver, the
phone rings again.*) Yes?

v.o.: Your son has called twice with a message, sir.

51

JOCK: I see. Well, I have to be at the airport. Would you order
    me a cab? Oh, and my bags are ready.
V.O.: Yes, sir.

56. INT. JOCK'S CAR   DAY
Heathrow-Hammersmith early morning mist. TOM *is driving.*
JOCK: Ever been to Huntingdon, Tom?
TOM: No, sir. I haven't actually.
JOCK: No. Well, I suppose you might.
TOM: Never know, sir.

57. INT. HOSPITAL PRIVATE ROOM   DAY
JOCK *is in bed. His* WIFE *is visiting him. A silent television is on.
They both glance at it from each other.*
JOCK: I think this is almost the noisiest place I've been in.
LADY MELLOR: They always are.
JOCK: People dodging all the way down the corridor. God
    knows what. Flannel faces and wool dressing-gowns and
    plastic bags and nurses giggling and clanging kidney basins
    and trolleys and sour-tempered coloured cleaners and
    rubber boots. All that . . . I'd almost forgotten it. Have
    you seen the old man?
LADY MELLOR: No. Do you think it's a good idea—to go on
    television?
JOCK: No. Still, I doubt I'll get to Huntingdon. Or Filey, or
    Barmouth.
LADY MELLOR: What?
JOCK: Could you pass me that other pillow? Thanks. They do
    this best.
LADY MELLOR: Yes. I suppose they do.

58. INT. TELEVISION STUDIO   DAY
TELEVISION INTERVIEWER *is interrogating* JOCK.
T.V. INTERVIEWER: You have, presumably, thought about these
    matters carefully. . . .
JOCK: No. I don't think I have. I just started out as a pretty
    simple engineer, you see. Concrete pipes.

T.V. INTERVIEWER: Yes.

JOCK: So. It shows you——

T.V. INTERVIEWER: What?

JOCK: If that's what concrete pipes can do to you——

T.V. INTERVIEWER: Sir Jock, you've raised these questions and we've discussed some of them, can I now ask you:

JOCK: How does one avoid cruelty and still survive?

T.V. INTERVIEWER: That seems a pretty rhetorical question. Are you expecting an answer—from me?

JOCK: No. I don't believe in, in power, in your power, my power, but, there, some of us, have a bit of it. But to *believe* in it, now, can you think of *anyone* saying "we are the masters now". Yes—you can. So can I. I still hear them. All right. I believe in getting the country on its feet; showing *them* what *we* can do. Thirty per cent more refrigerators; that Britain can still *lead*, leaders of industry and the powers of negotiation, the struggle against imperialism abroad; that for those in what was once the twilight of life there is new hope; they might even reach the commanding British heights of the Common Market; of paying our way, pulling in and letting out our belts—I've done it all my life anyway (so have you); doing your own things in your own jumbo airport, *not*, repeat *not* being outmoded, out of date but streamlined. Everything will be *new*, constructive, forward-looking. There will be, there will be—no today. Only tomorrow. *I* know. I *made* it. We will live in a vast village that is always just about to exist because the present is pretty—*quite* unthinkable. . . . (*Scramble in studio.*)

T.V. INTERVIEWER: I see. And—then—what *about* the present?

JOCK: Oh—— Very like. Like a Whale.

(*He gets up to go.* TELEVISION INTERVIEWER *to another camera.*)

T.V. INTERVIEWER: Thank you, Sir Jock. Later in the programme, I shall be talking to some leading industrialists, Sir Percy Spencer, the Minister for Home and Overseas Development, two Senior Trade Unionists. . . .

(JOCK *is collapsing in the corner of the studio during all of this. Technicians watch as people try to help him to his feet.*)

59. INT. FLAT   NIGHT

JOCK'*s father is preparing* SAM'*s dinner.* SAM *is watching the news.*

NEWSCASTER: Eleven of the demonstrators were later charged with obstructing the police and three with possession of offensive weapons. . . . Sir Jock Mellor, leading industrialist and pioneer of labour techniques and all manner of advancement in the fields of engineering and technology died this evening at the end of a television interview. He had been in poor health for some time and only recently knighted for his services to international and industrial relations.

FATHER: Come on, Sam boy. Dinner time, then.

(SAM *goes on watching.*)

You don't want to watch that.

NEWSCASTER: He was forty-nine. . . .

(FATHER *switches over to the other channel.*)

FATHER: There we are then. We don't want the old thing, do we? Come on, then.

(SAM *eats out of his bowl.*)

There's a good boy. I knew you'd like *that*. Now what are we going to watch tonight? Eh? Let's have a look at the silly old papers. . . . What are we going to look at tonight? (SAM *eats.* FATHER *looks at the paper in the flicker of the screen.*)

CURTAIN

54